Dirty Words Coloring Book For Kids

By: J.S. Stewart

Dirty Words Coloring Book For Kids

By: J.S.Stewart

If you are reading this, you must be a cool kid! I mean, for an adult to buy you a book with dirty words... Shoot... You gotta be super cool. But, don't forget the thank that grown-up! Because they are so awesome that they bought you a coloring book called Dirty Words.

I bet your other friends don't have a book as cool as this. DANG! You gotta be special!

Well, anywho, I hope you enjoy these somewhat kid safe DIRTY WORDS! I had fun putting it together! Just remember. You are awesome and can do anything! Keep your mind creative and free thinking and you will move mountains and change the world. Thanks for being such a cool kid! Keep it up!

Maybe you'll get another one of these... Make sure to ask the same adult for it

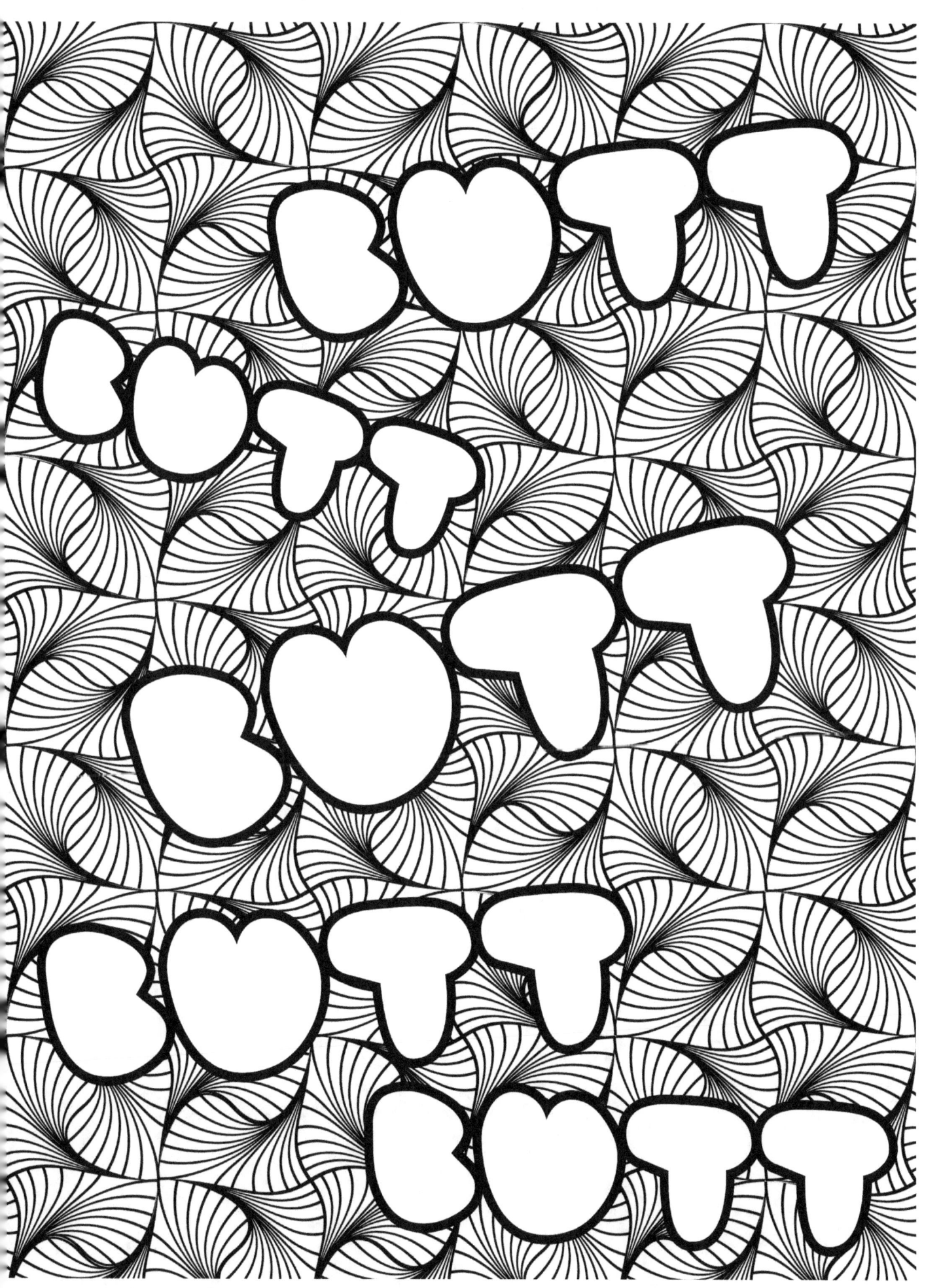

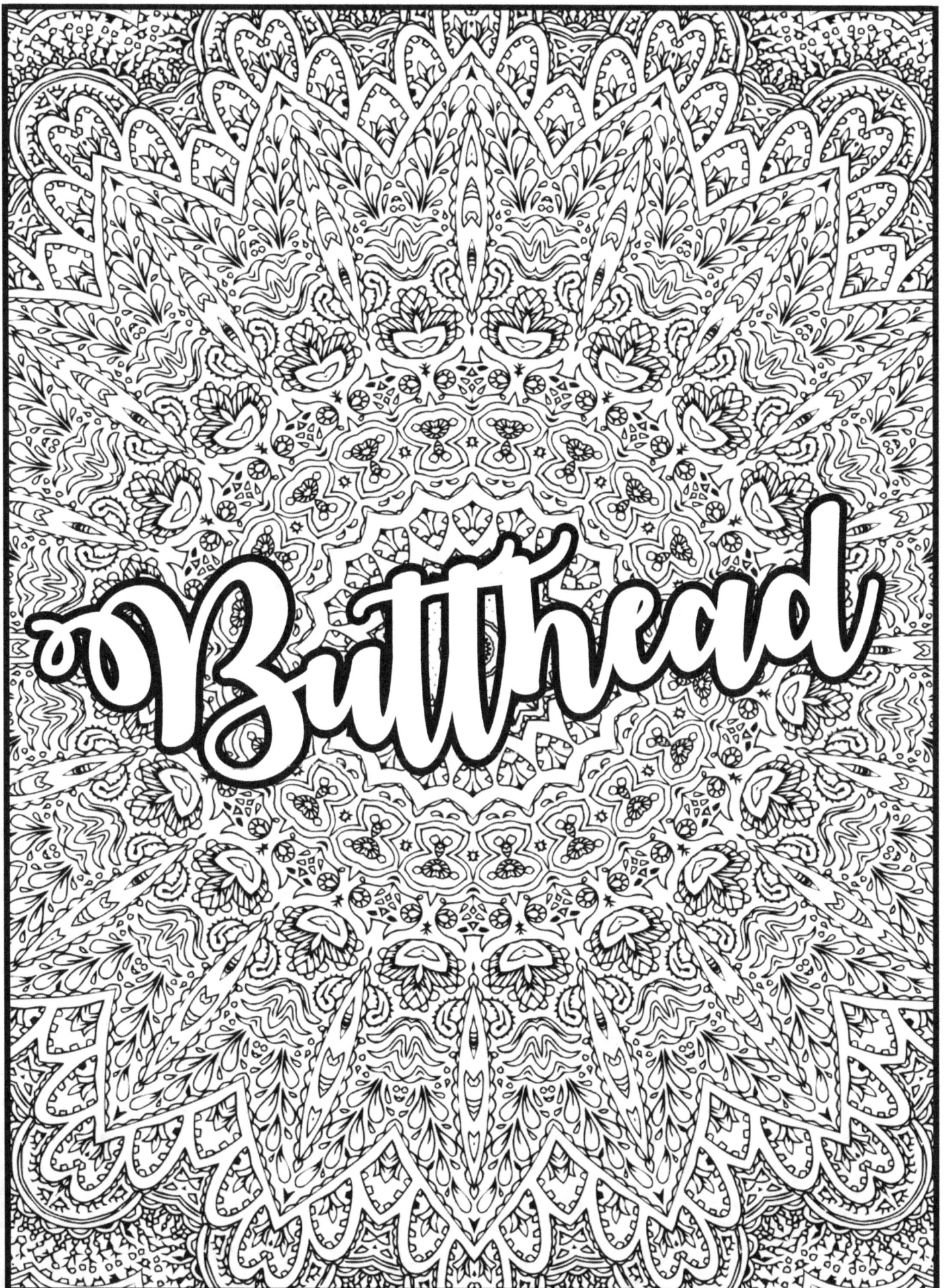

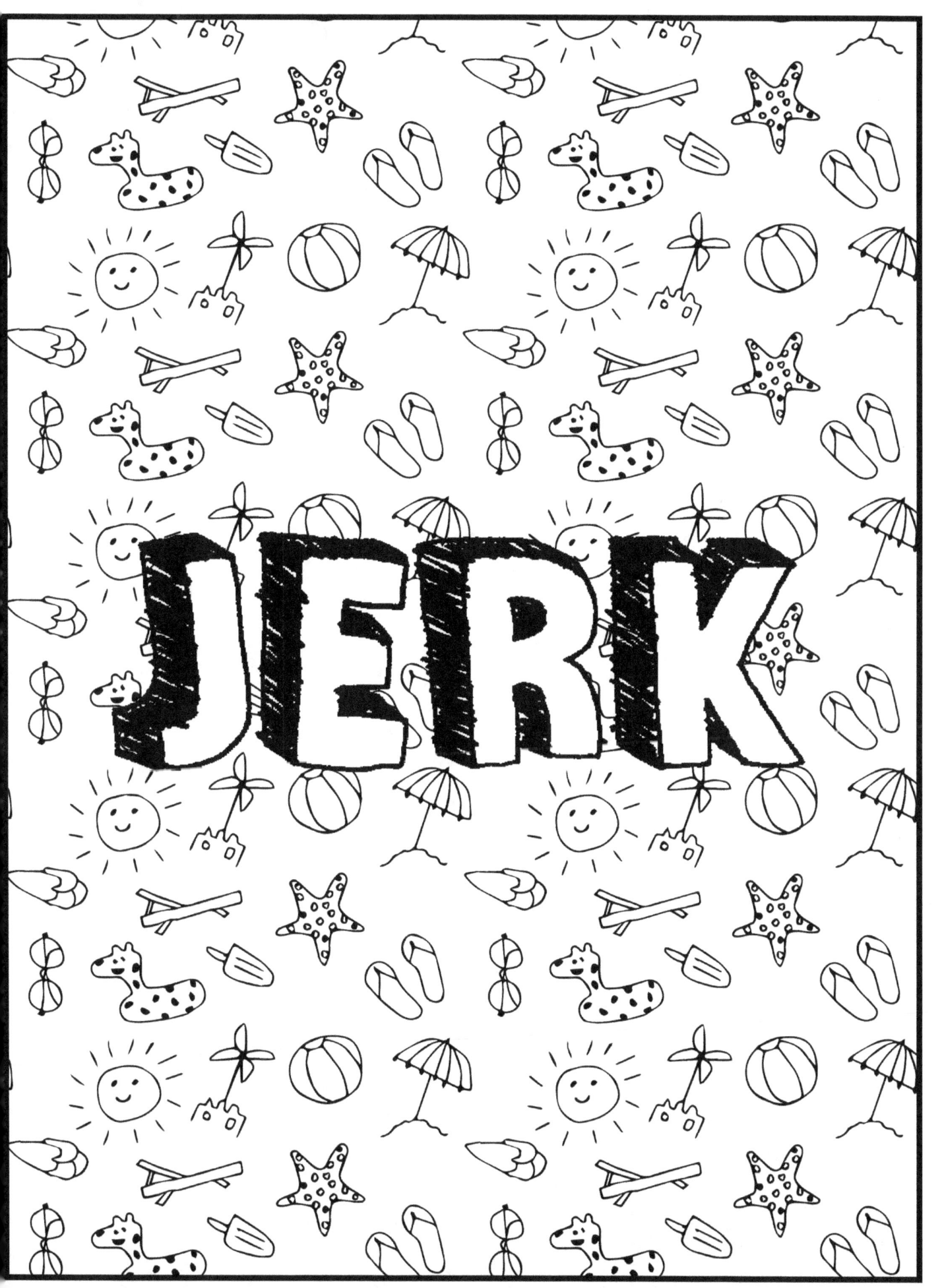

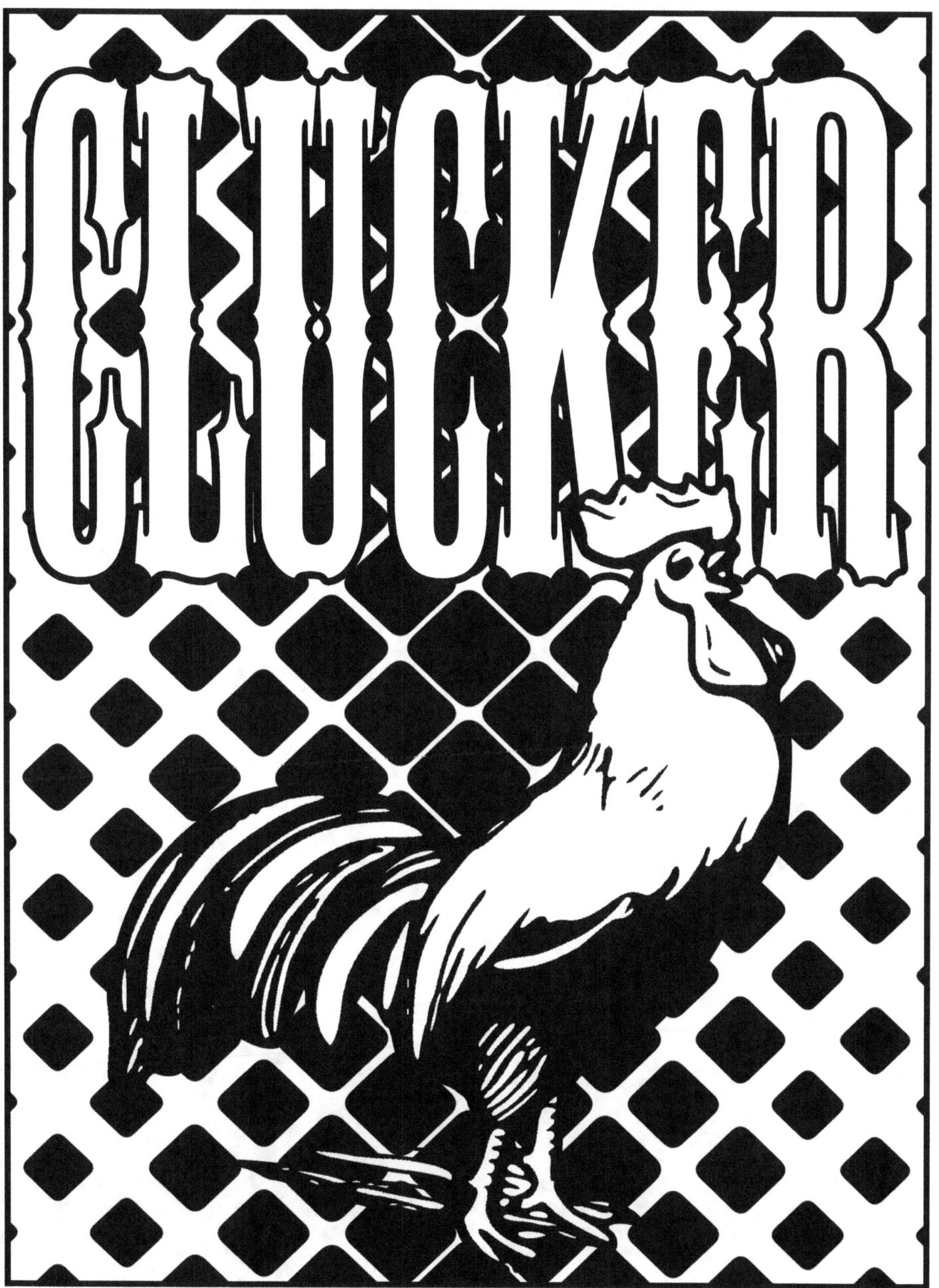

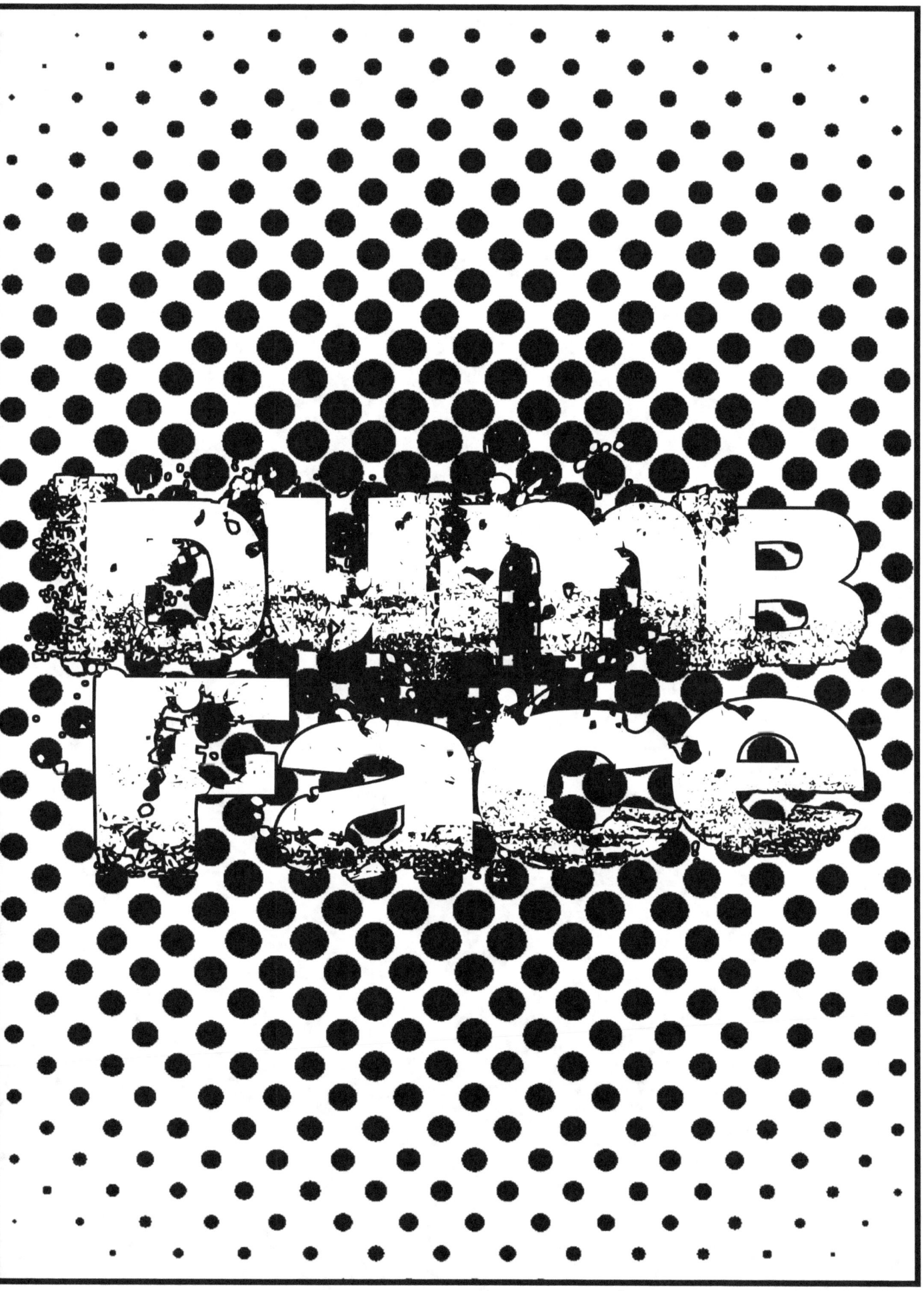

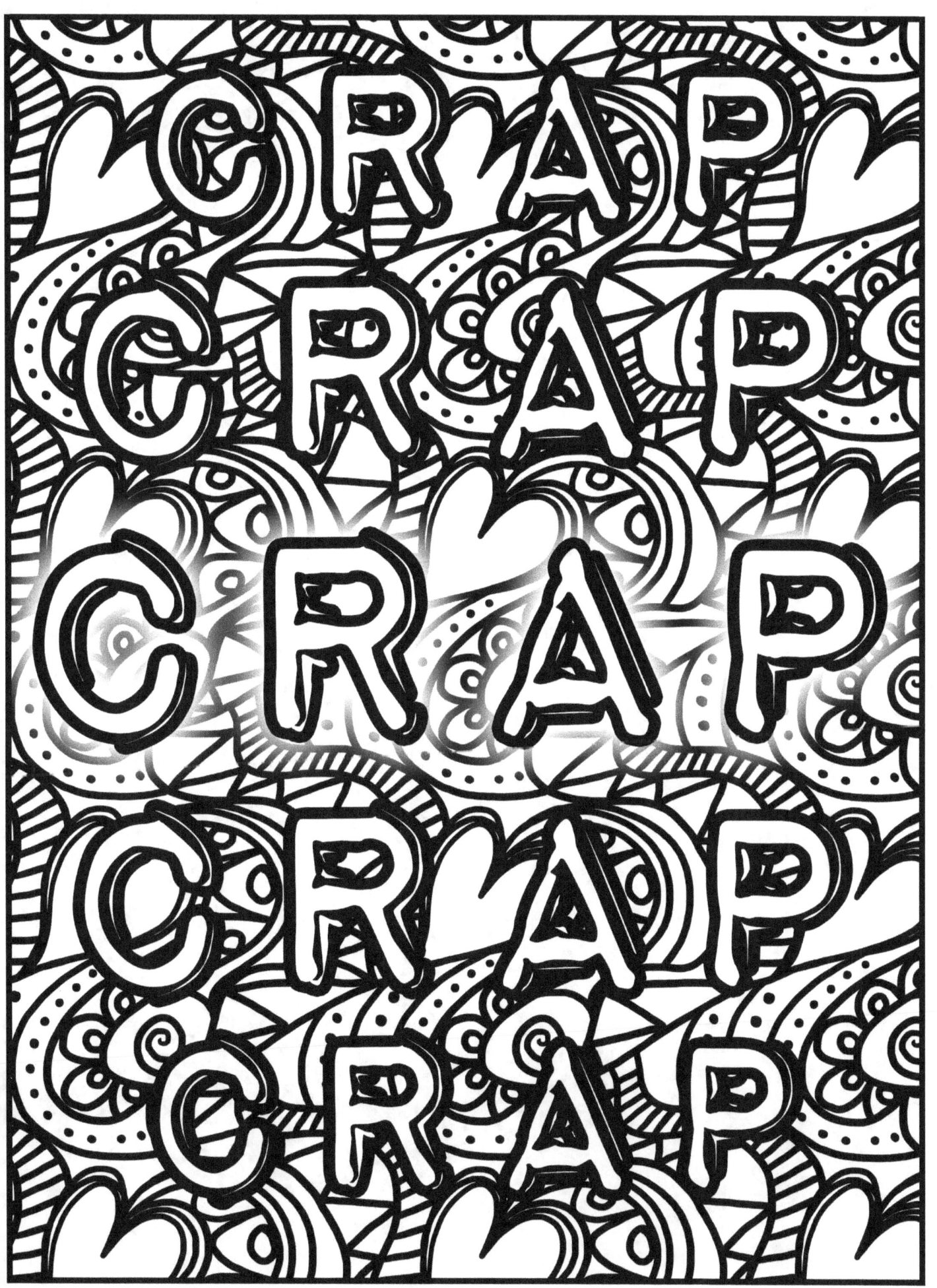

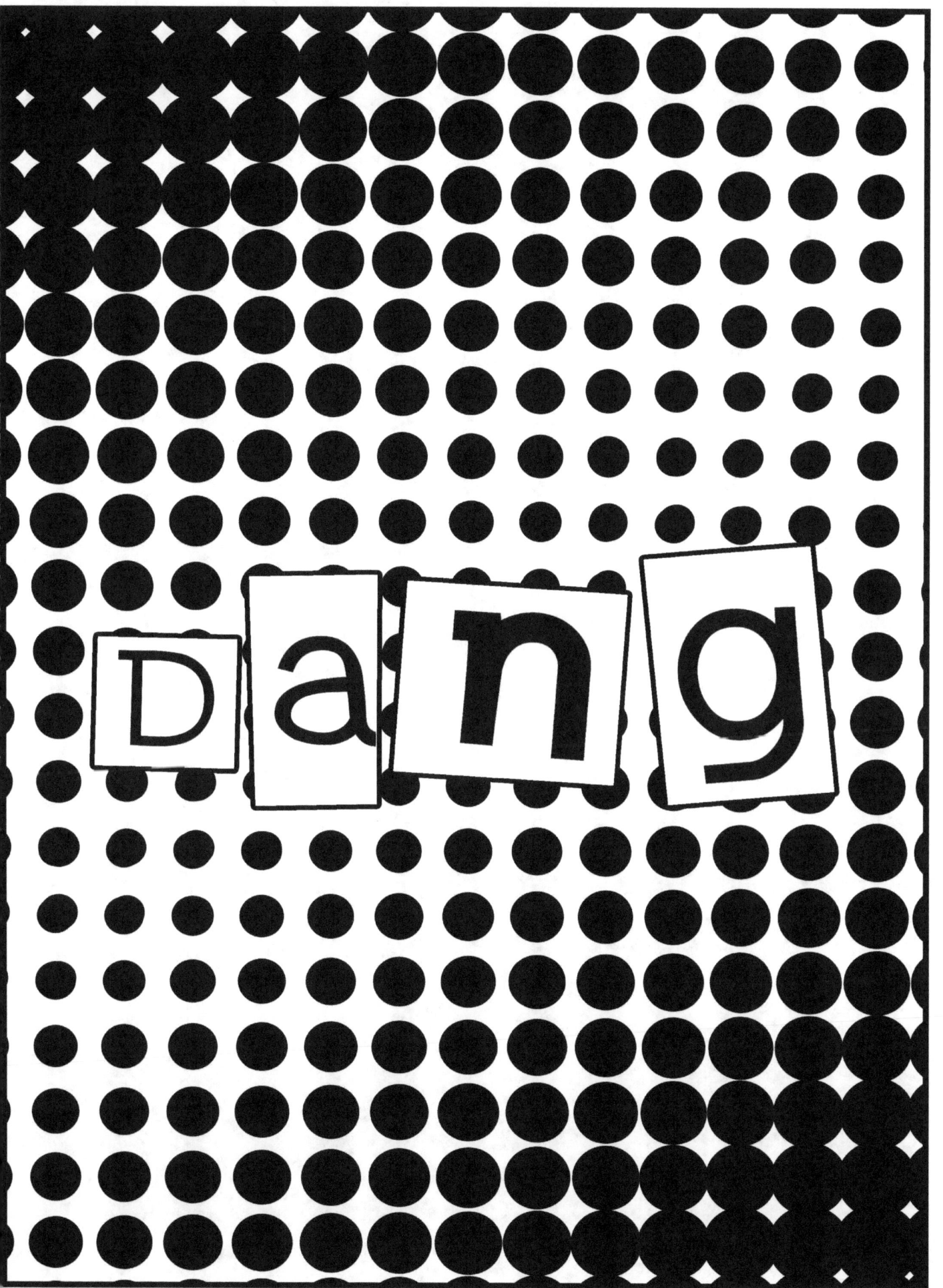

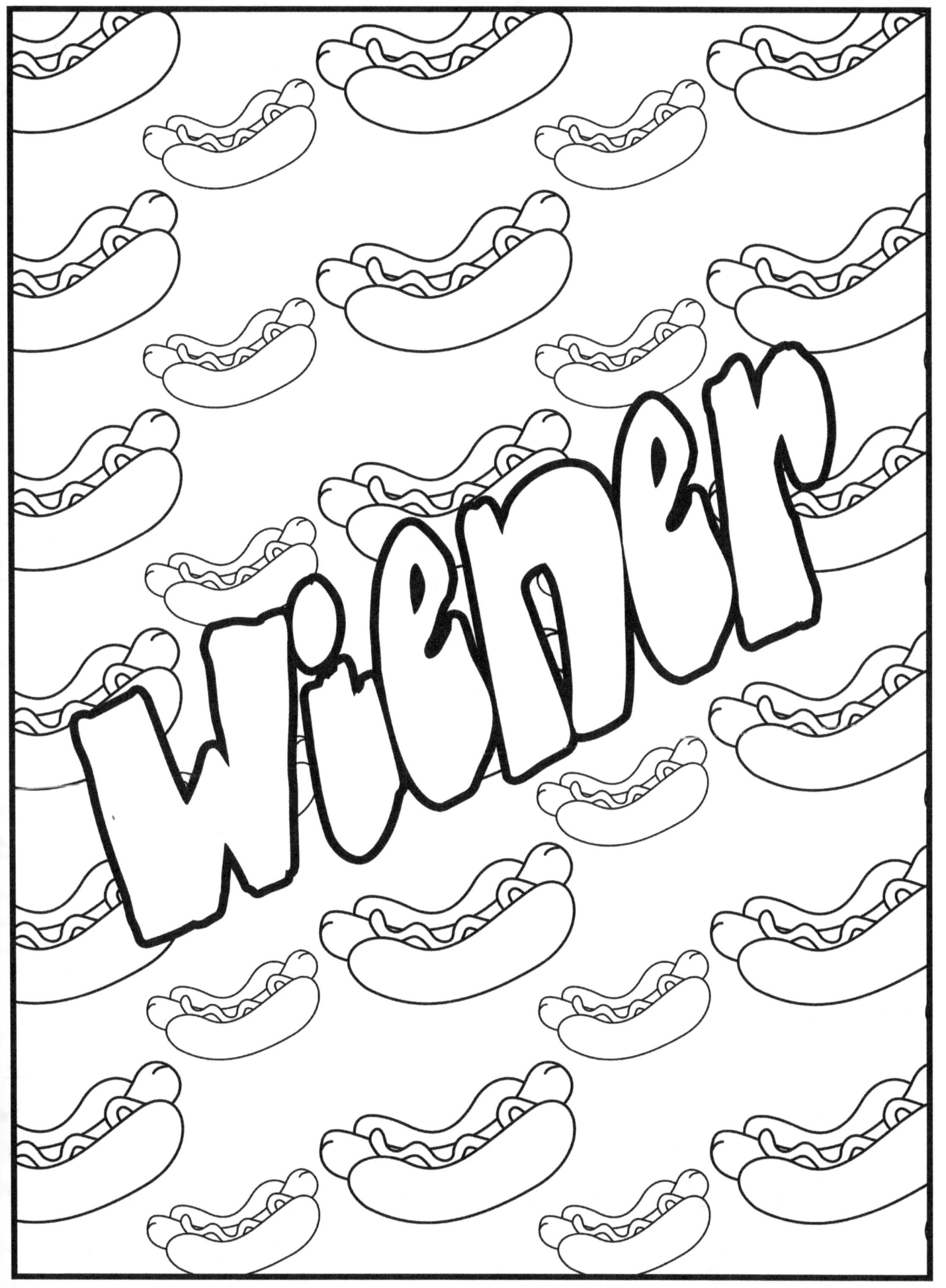

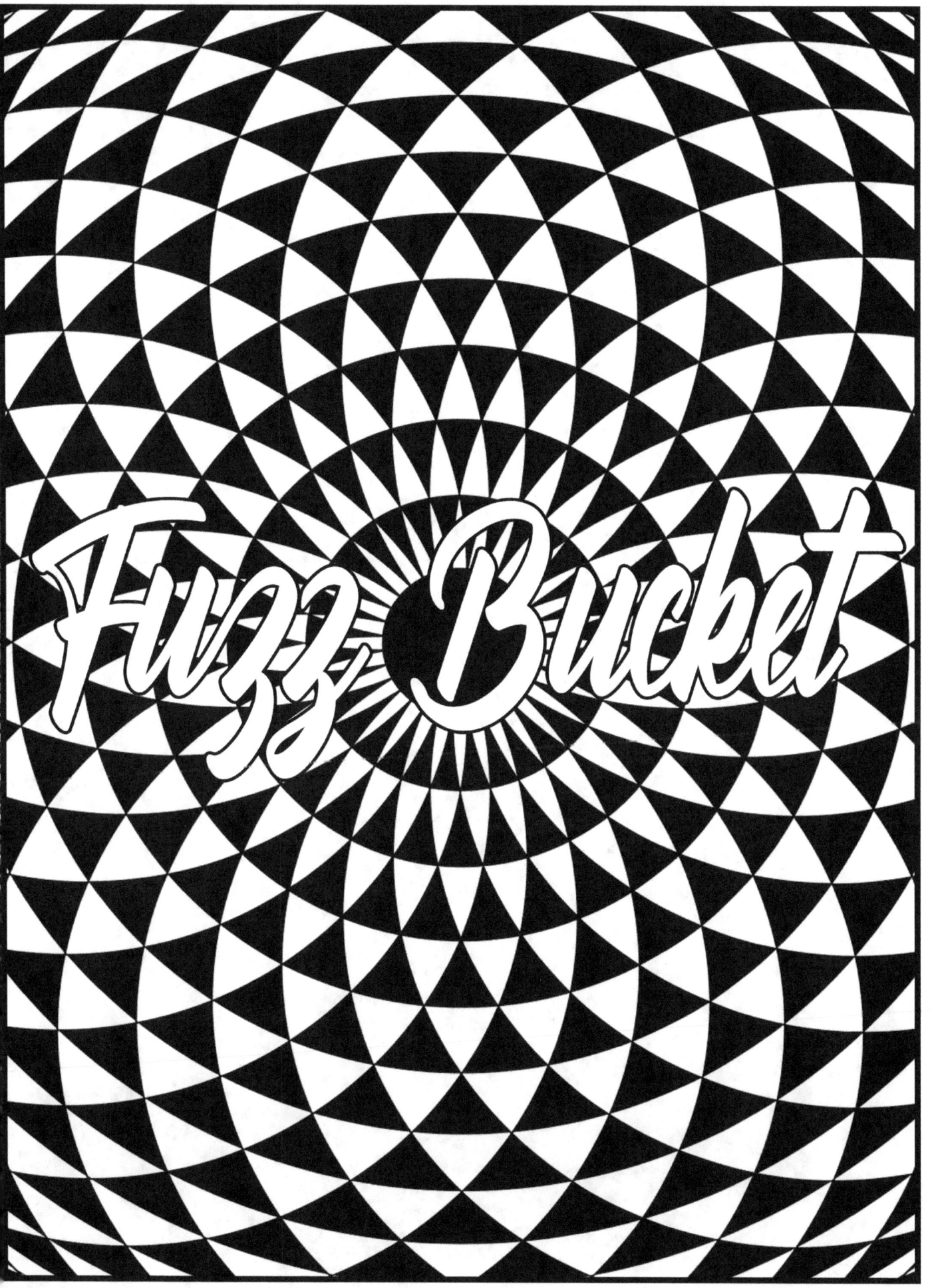

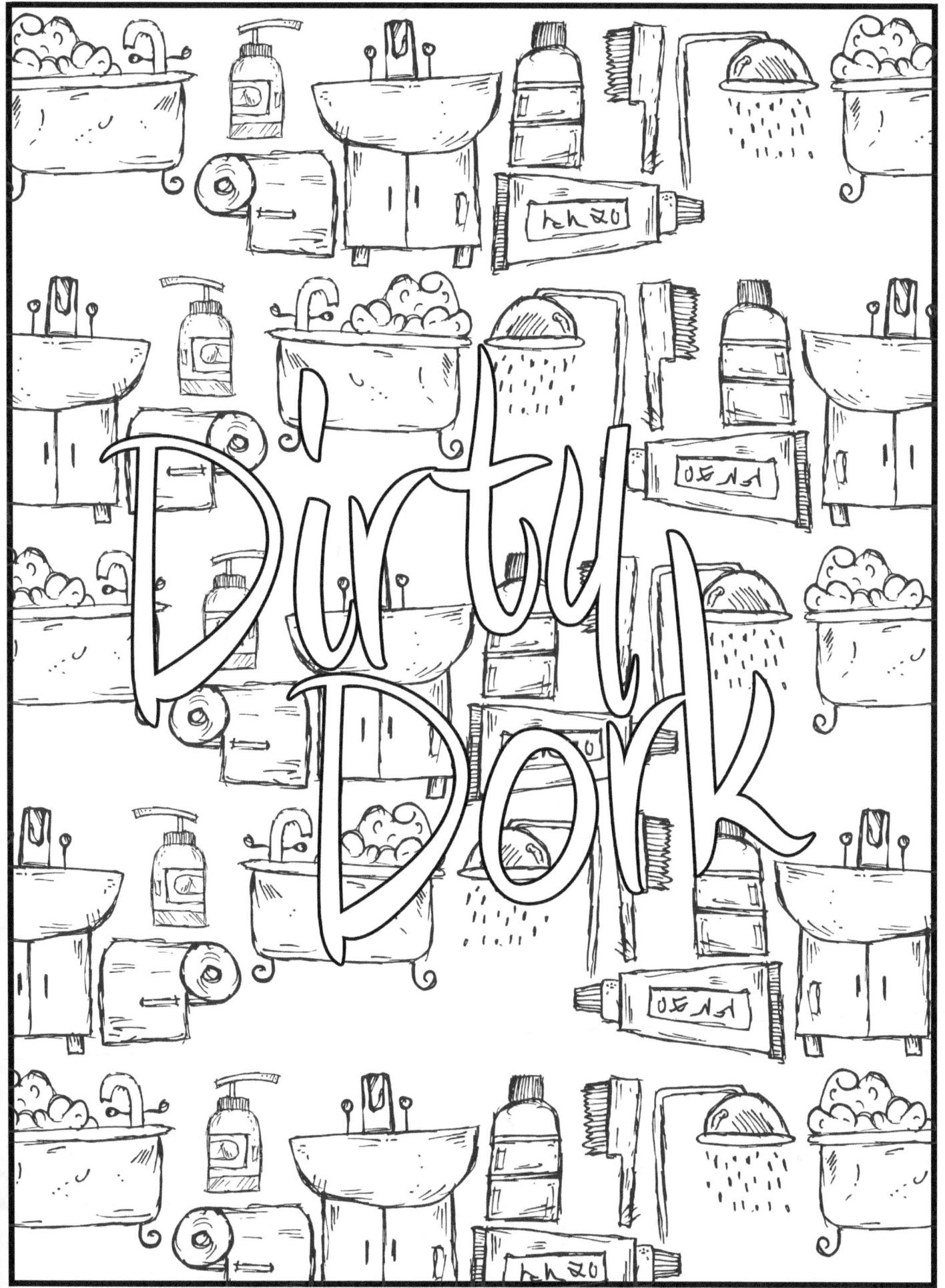

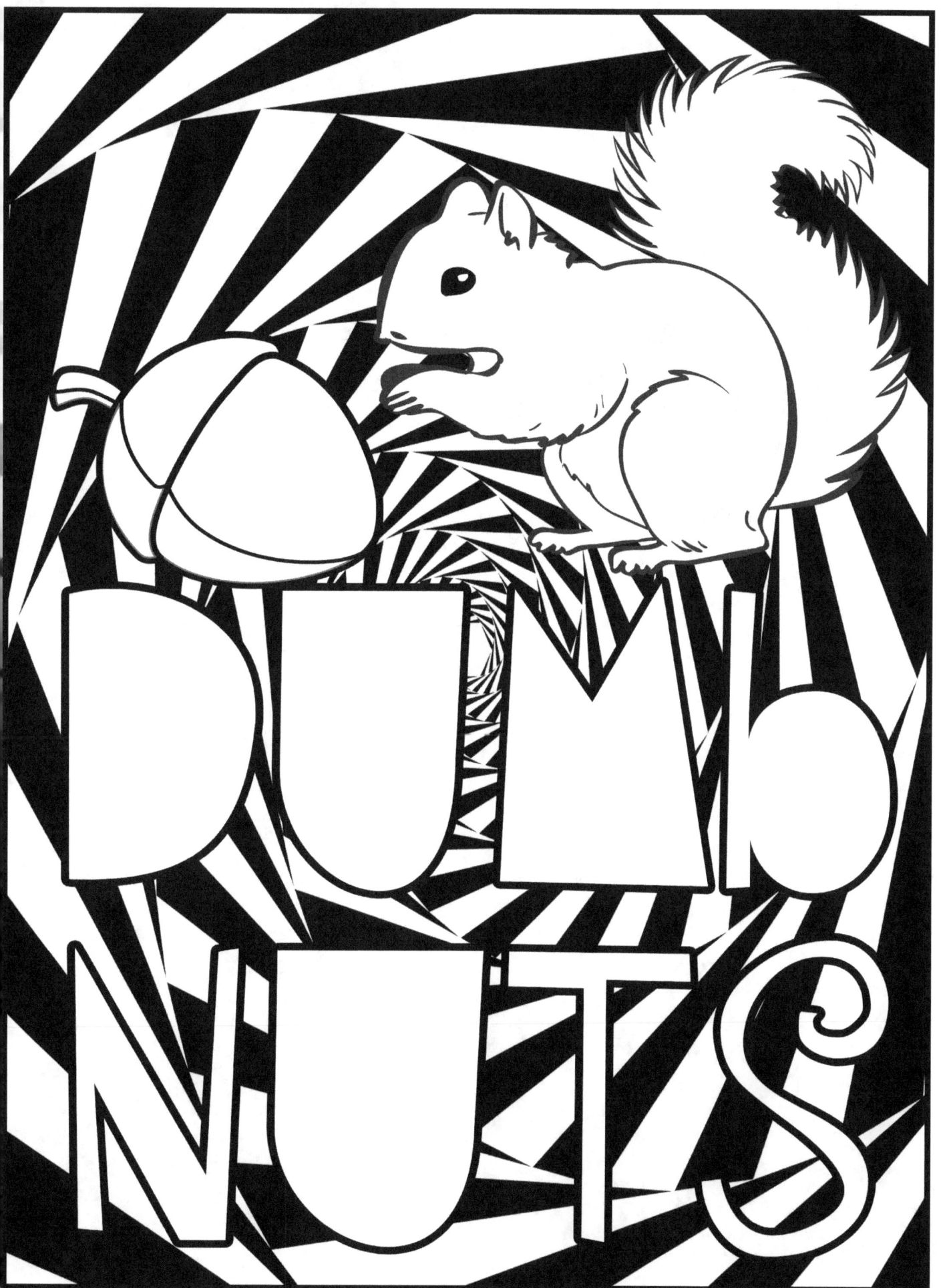

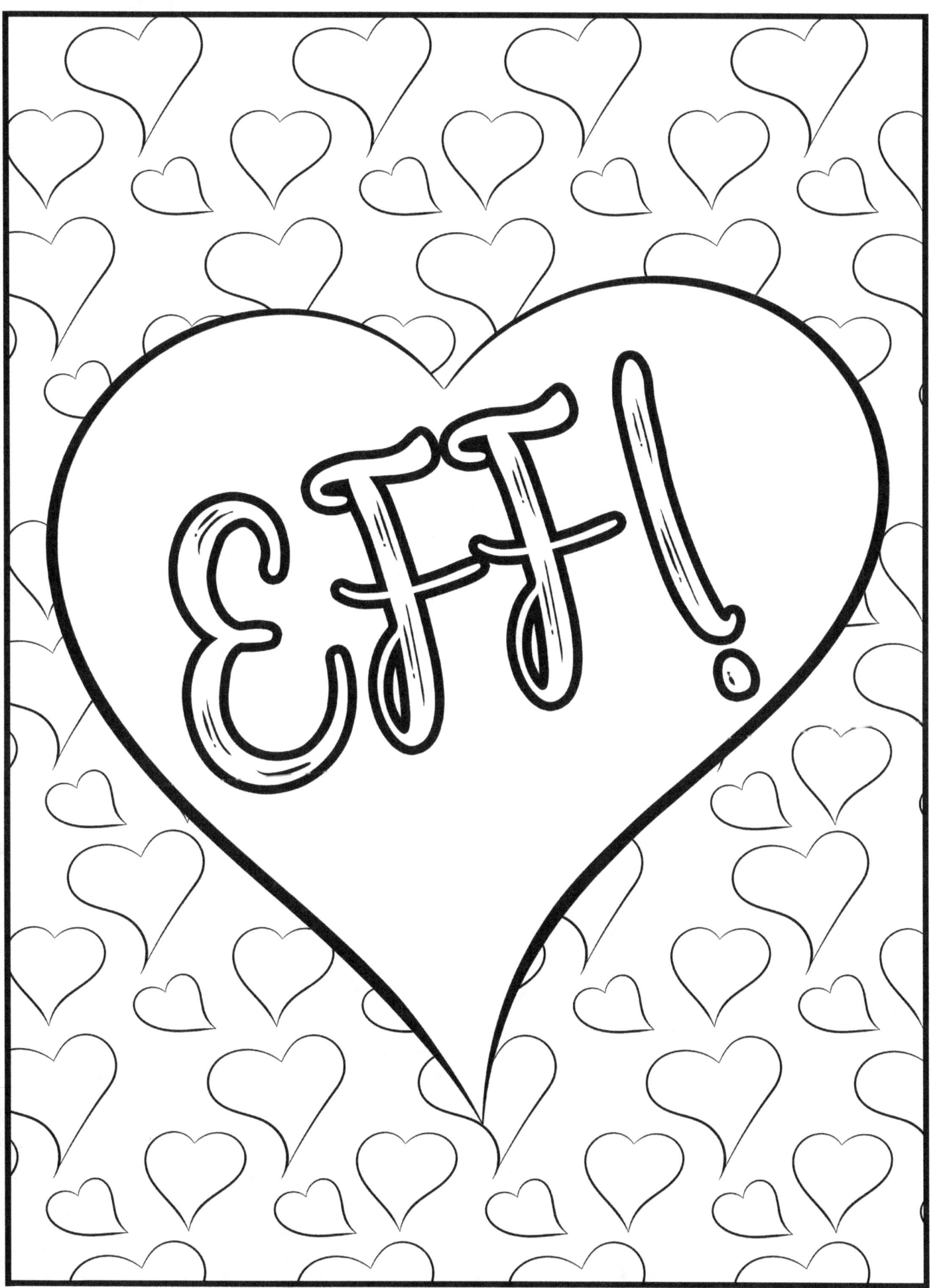

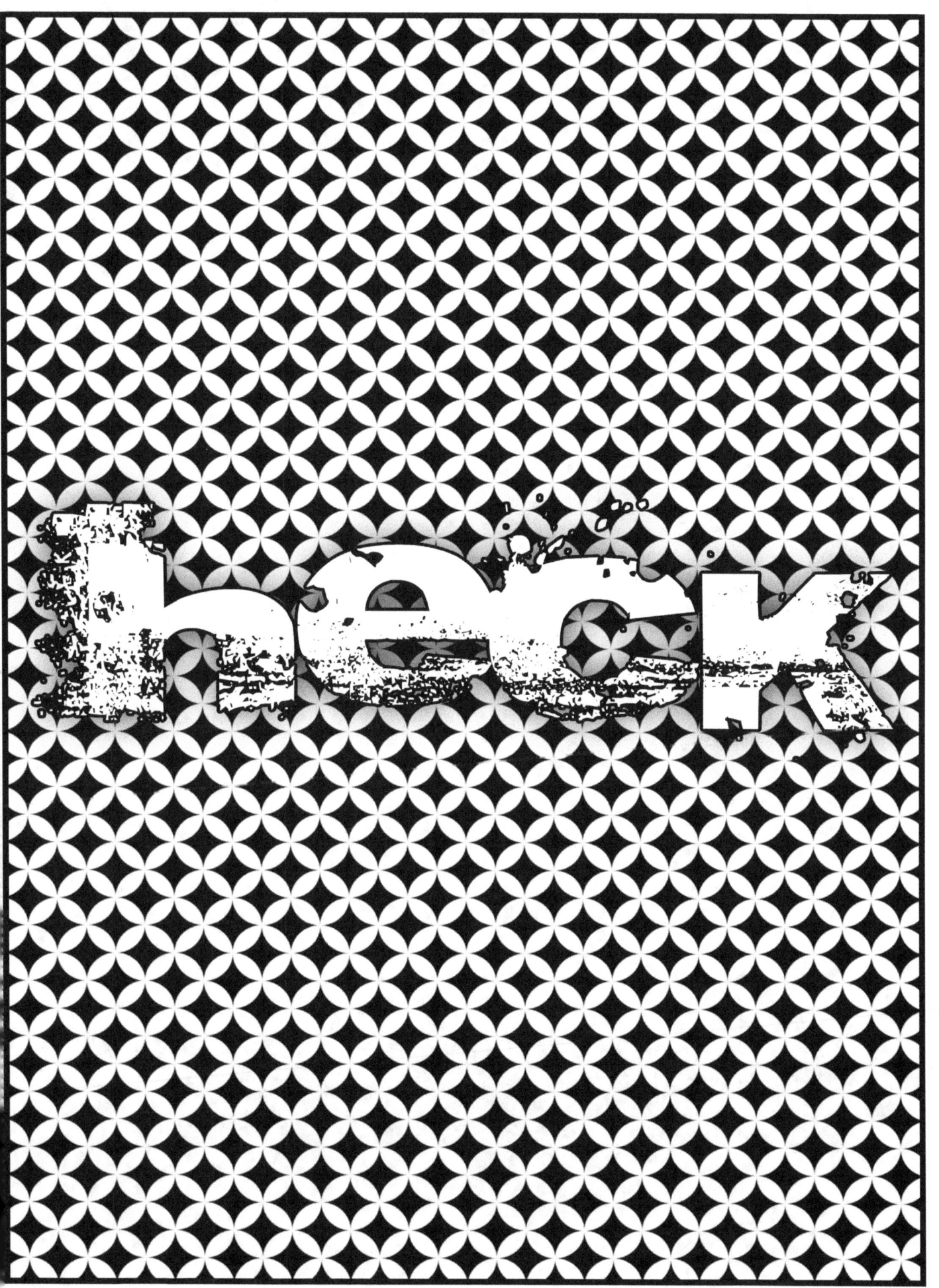

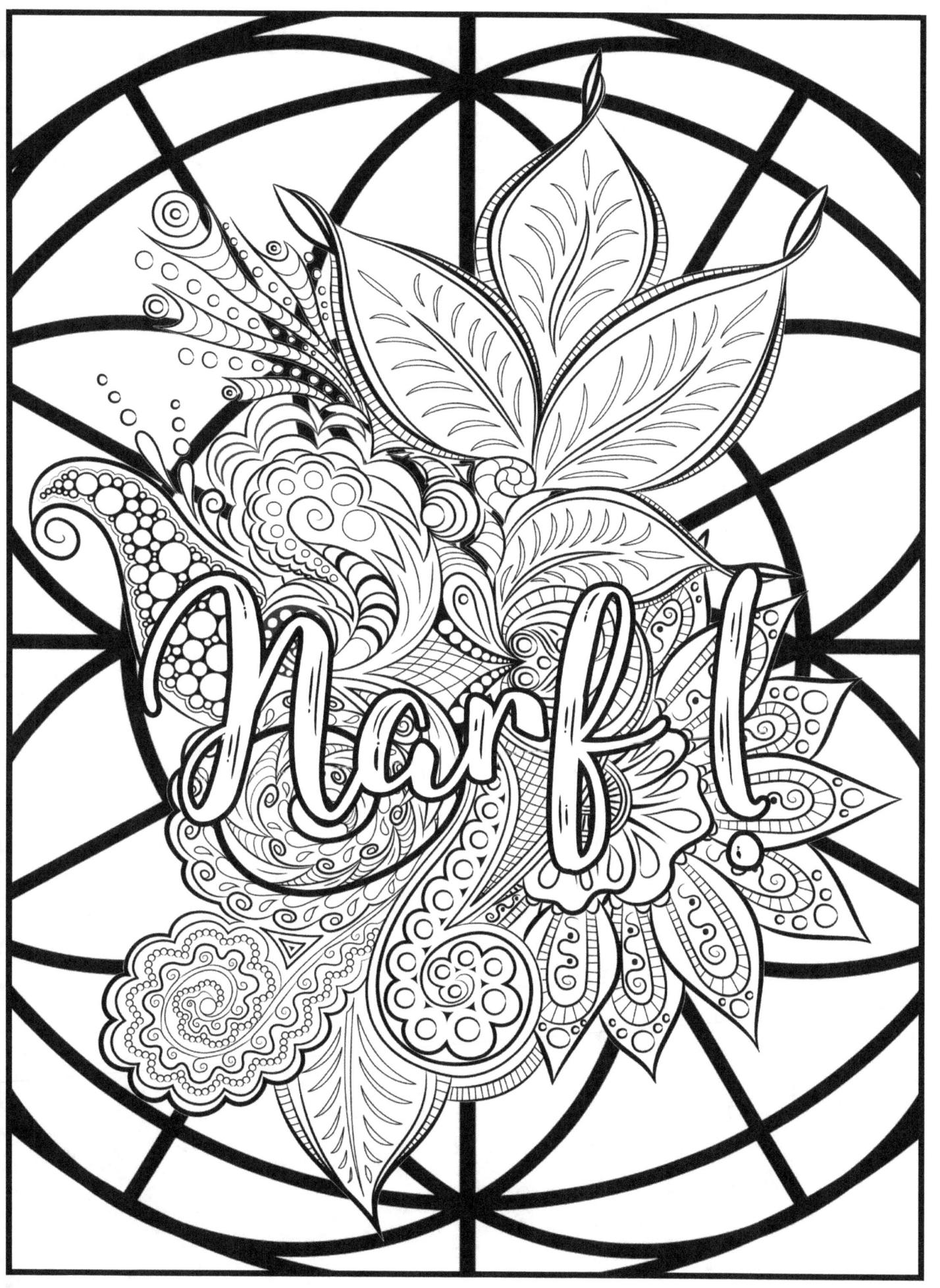

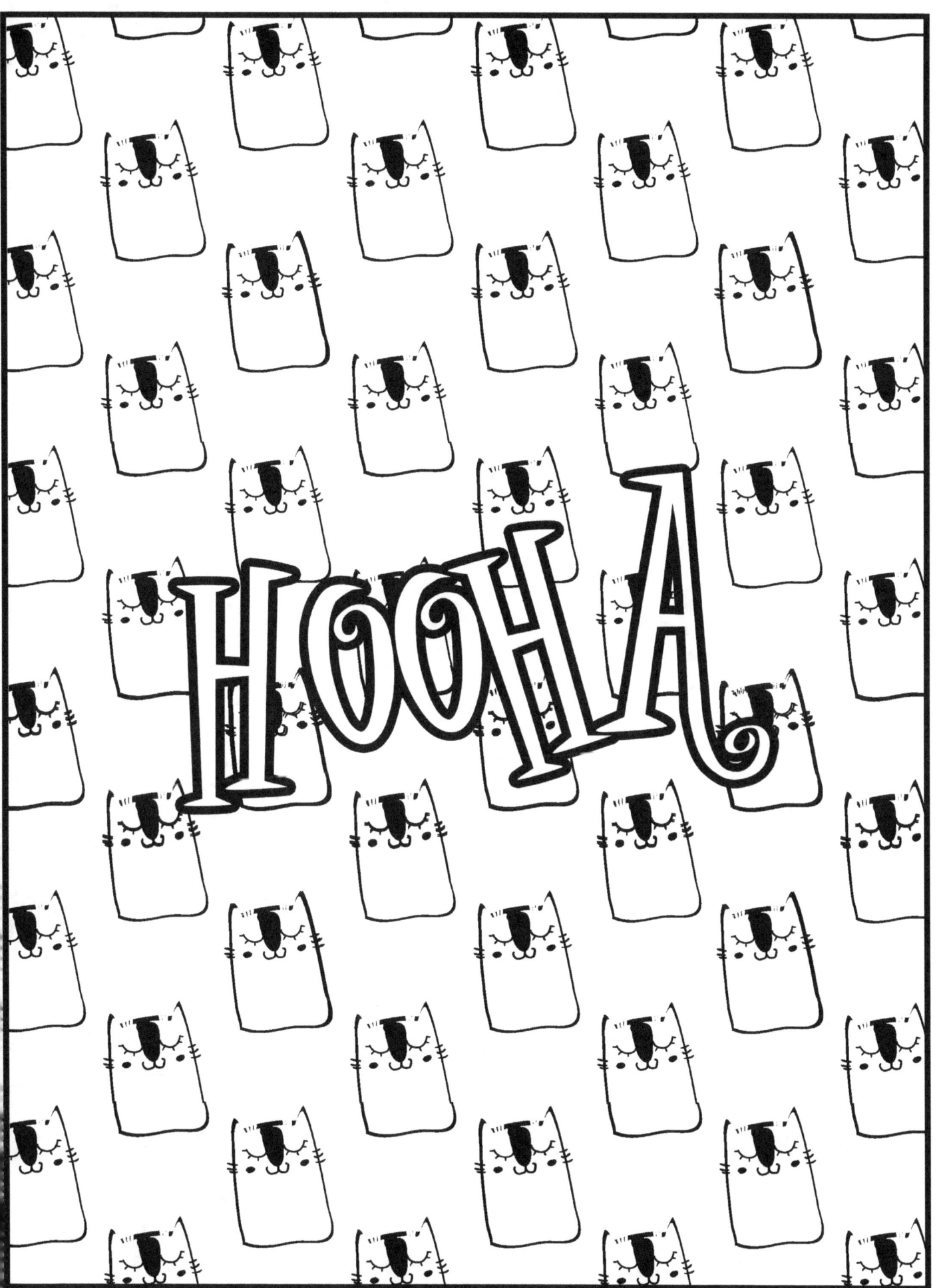

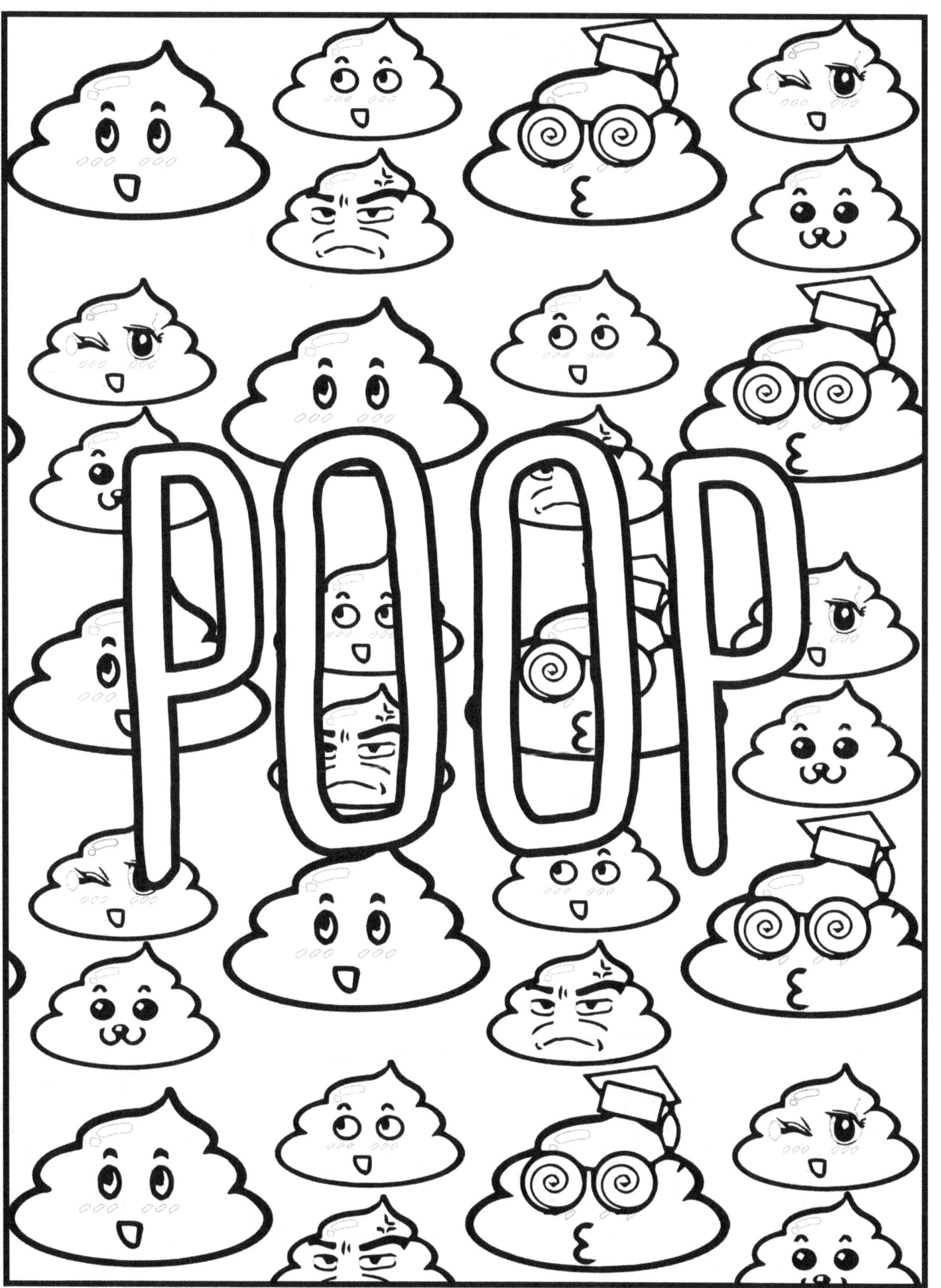

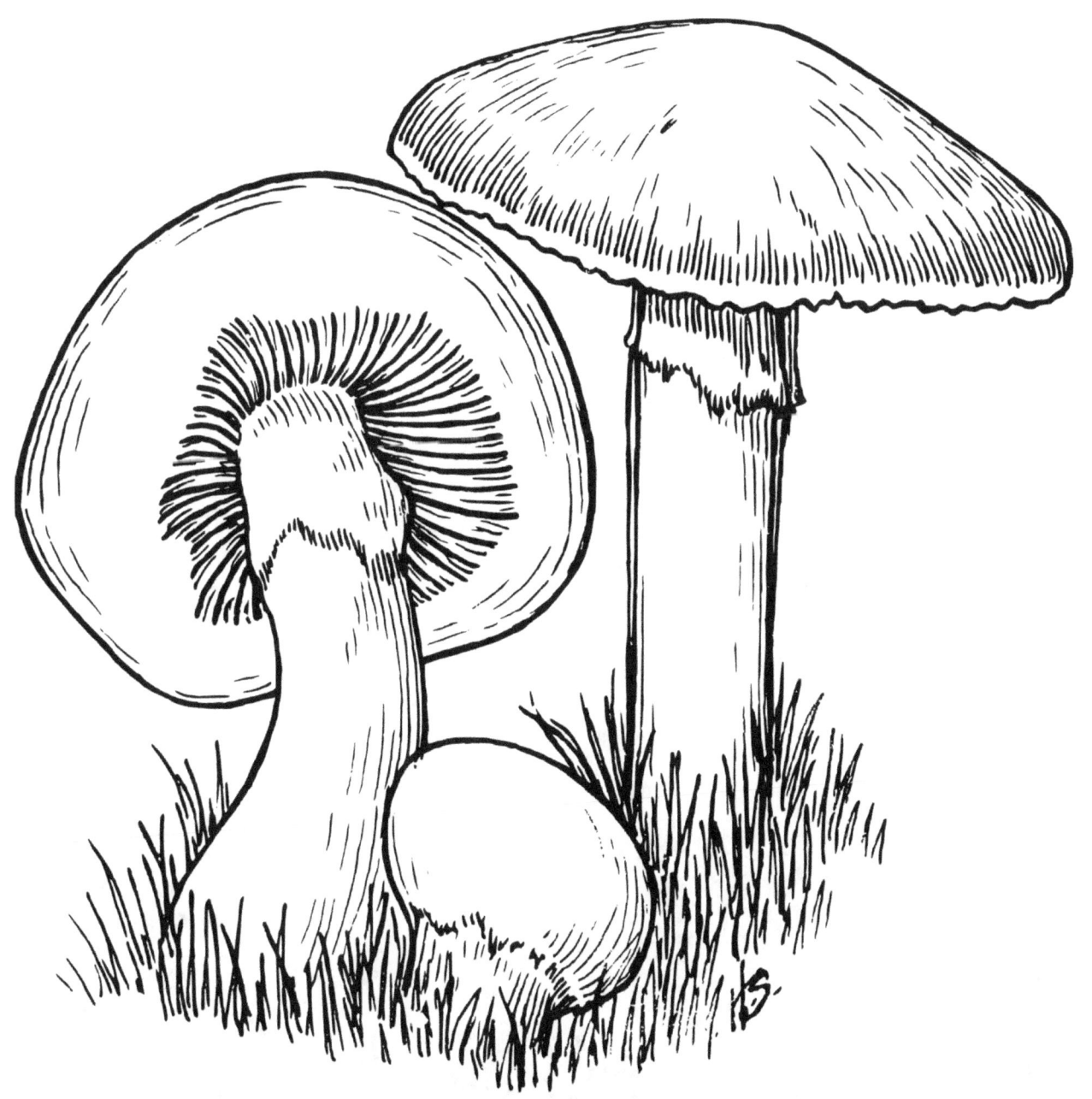

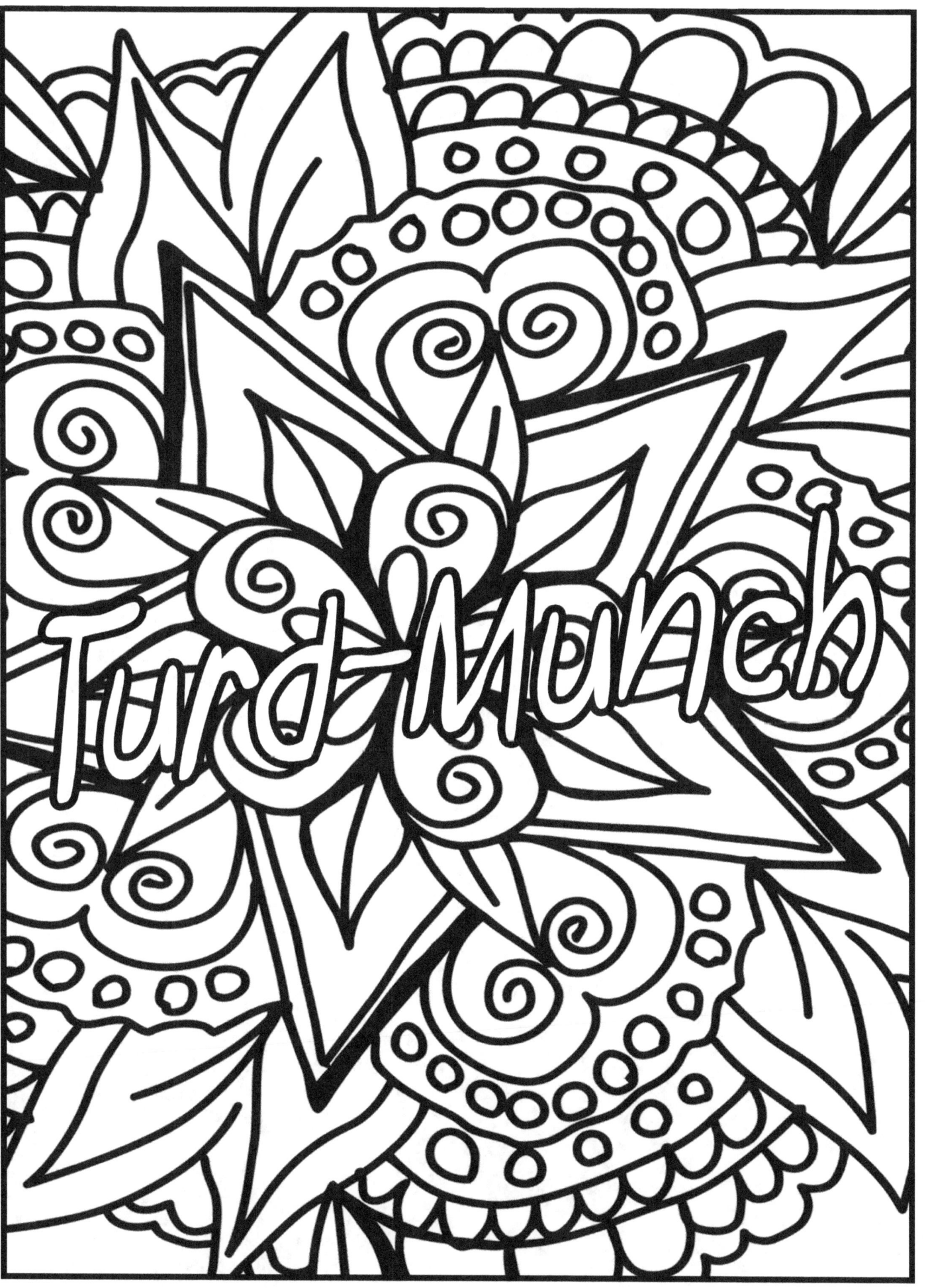

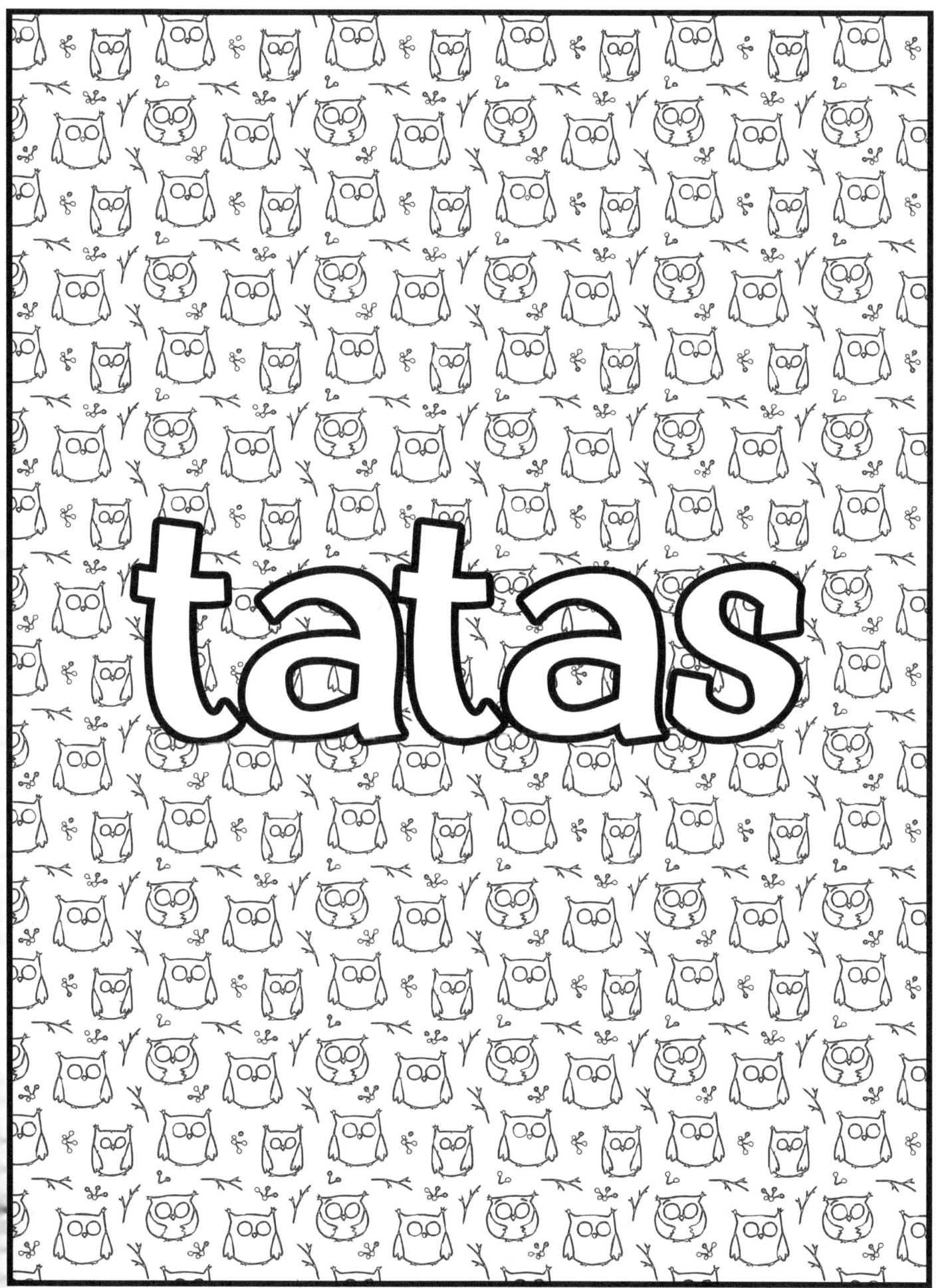

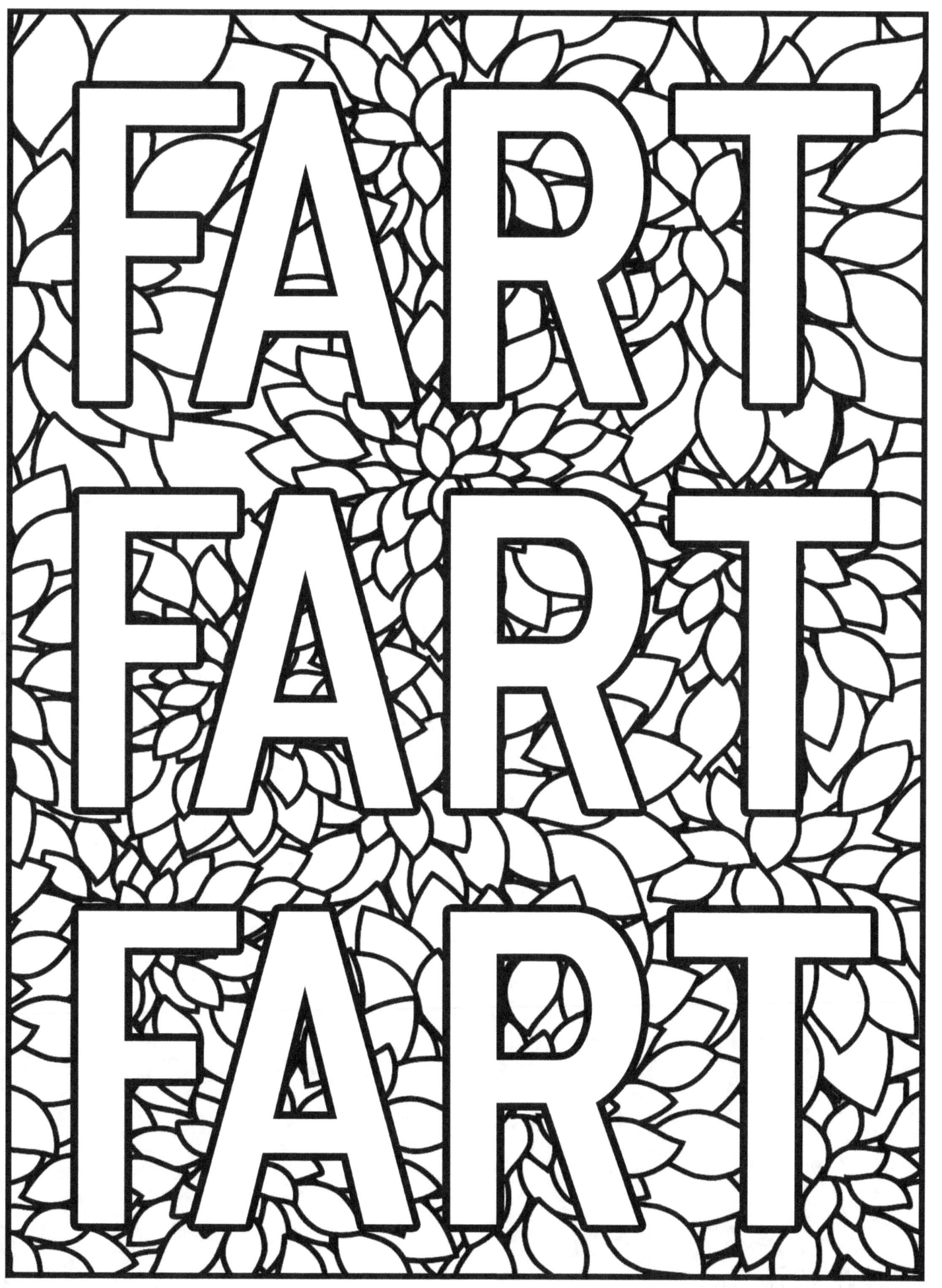

www.ingramcontent.com/pod-product-compliance
Lightning Source LLC
Chambersburg PA
CBHW081704220526
45466CB00009B/2877